D1161453

PRACTICAL LETTERING AND LAYOUT

PRACTICAL
LETTERING
& LAYOUT

By F.J.MITCHELL A.R.C.A
HEAD OF DEPARTMENT OF COMMERCIAL
ART AND ADVERTISING DESIGN AT THE
HORNSEY SCHOOL OF ART AND CRAFTS

WITH TWENTY
TWO FULL-PAGE
ILLUSTRATIONS
BY THE AUTHOR

A. & C. BLACK LTD
4,5 & 6 SOHO SQUARE, LONDON, W.1

The United States
THE MACMILLAN COMPANY, NEW YORK

Australia and New Zealand
THE OXFORD UNIVERSITY PRESS, MELBOURNE

Canada
THE MACMILLAN COMPANY OF CANADA, TORONTO

South Africa
THE OXFORD UNIVERSITY PRESS, CAPE TOWN

India, Burma, China and F.M.S.
MACMILLAN AND COMPANY, LIMITED
BOMBAY   CALCUTTA   MADRAS

FIRST PUBLISHED 1935

MADE AND PRINTED IN GREAT BRITAIN BY
BILLING AND SONS LIMITED, GUILDFORD AND ESHER

INTRODUCTION

In planning this book, I have had uppermost in my mind the idea of constructing a lettering book which will help the beginner in his task of overcoming the first steps towards good lettering and layout, and later will help him to produce good lettering for a practical purpose.

Considerable experience in teaching lettering has made me realize the necessity of having a definite method or system to simplify the approach to the subject. It must be understood that all lettering is a form of design, and if *layout design* is made the foundation of lettering the production of letter-forms becomes of fascinating interest because they are units of a creative design. While it is absolutely necessary to study good basic types of letters before attempting to create new types, the best way of learning them 'without tears' is to make them an exercise in creative layout.

This book has been written and illustrated especially as an aid to the acquisition of an appreciation of lettering and a knowledge of practical methods of letter-production, and it is hoped that it will be of value as a systematic course of study for use in schools.

Special sections of the book are devoted to the production of lettering and layout related to the requirements of ticket writing for shop display and for commercial advertising. We are confronted daily with all types of lettering from the morning newspaper to the last book at night. It is more than ever an essential vehicle of thought in our modern civilization. Thousands must be concerned with its use in business, yet how many realize that good and bad lettering can have a powerful influence on the spectator and on business sales? If this book can help to produce good lettering, then it will justify itself.

F. J. M.

CONTENTS

2

I. ESSENTIALS OF GOOD LETTERING

First and foremost it should be realized that all lettering is a form of design, and should be approached from this angle. There is no justification for bad lettering; by an understanding of the simple fundamentals which govern the production of all lettering, poor lettering should be impossible. The main essentials of good lettering may be summarized as follows:

Quality, which may vary in degree according to
1. The skill of the craftsman in the use of his tools.
2. The form and suitability of the type of lettering for its purpose.
3. The arrangement or layout, dependent on the creative ability of the designer.

Legibility, an obvious factor which is nevertheless often absent through such faults as overcrowding, confusion with other decoration or pictorial matter, letter-forms that are too exaggerated or fantastic, or bad choice of colour. Remember always that readableness is the chief consideration.

Style, beauty and character of letter. Each letter should have a beauty of its own. The following pages give examples of basic types to be studied, which will enable the designer to appreciate a new form of letter and will help him to create new and sound forms of letters of good character.

Letter-spacing, or the careful grouping together of letters to form words, resulting in unity.

Use of colour and tone values are interesting essentials which must be considered in conjunction with foundations of layout and arrangement.

Layout and arrangement. The first question that arises in the production of any lettering, however simple, is How is it to be arranged? The answer can either make or mar the work. Letters and words have to be considered as units or symbols to be planned into a design or pattern that will be legible and pleasing and fitted to the purpose for which it is intended.

II. LAYOUT OR MASS DESIGN: SIMPLE LAYOUT

Let us first consider the word Layout, which means the planning of the arrangement of words and pictorial matter to form a pleasing design as a finished whole.

If words and groups of words can be seen in mass or black areas, pleasing arrangements can be made unhampered by formation of individual letters. An excellent plan for the beginner, before considering the making of letters, is to construct and design simple silhouettes formed of rectangles and other geometric shapes similar to those illustrated opposite. The following exercises are designed to help the student to understand and prepare layout before studying the problems of letter-formation.

THE SILHOUETTES A AND B are examples of the simplest forms of *symmetrically balanced layout* in which the block or mass consists of a rectangle with arms or projections of equal length and size, so that the complete shape is evenly distributed on either side of an imaginary centre line. This type of layout is very straightforward and quite easy for the beginner to understand.

THE EXAMPLES C E D AND F are still balanced, not rigidly symmetrical as A and B, but allowing for rather more freedom in the arrangement of rectangular shapes. While the main masses have contrasting projections it will be noticed that in each little example there is a feeling of balance and a pleasing unity, brought about by careful planning of the lighter masses in relation to the heavier mass.

Many different and interesting effects can be obtained by simple planning in this way. Several of these layouts are the basis of finished examples of lettering to be found later in the book.

EXAMPLES OF EXERCISES IN LAYOUT DESIGN

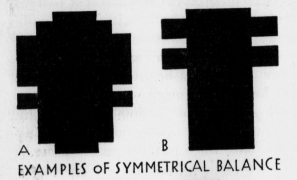

A   B

EXAMPLES OF SYMMETRICAL BALANCE

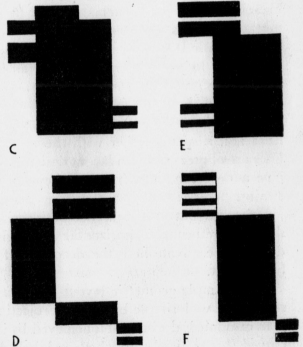

C   E

D   F

EXAMPLES OF BALANCED LAY-OUT·RECTANGLES OF VARYING SIZE

III. LAYOUT OR MASS DESIGN: GEOMETRICAL SHAPES

The student is advised to progress in this method of pattern making with rectangular shapes by introducing easily made units, such as lines, curves, spots and other simple geometric shapes. At first the patterns should be made with a black-lead pencil or ink, later they should be attempted in colour, preferably in poster colour, commencing with simple colour harmonies such as one colour and black, then experimenting with fuller ranges of colour. This will be found a fascinating study and of great value later when put into practical use.

EXAMPLE A illustrates an exercise introducing the effect of a mass, together with lighter areas and line. This is a simple method of relief and decoration in layout and adds to the interest while keeping the whole quite geometric.

In B the interesting mass is still retained but placed at an angle, thus giving an unusual appearance without the aid of line.

C is an example of what can be achieved by the use of lines and a spot together with the main block. Spots and lines are of great value in layout designs, for they immediately give a decorative quality—but they must be used with restraint.

D is a layout of a very decorative character, triangular shapes together with horizontal rectangles and a perpendicular line. Note how the decorative feeling is enhanced by the spot.

E is a simple geometric layout with a mass formed into a semicircle, with simple block and projections.

In example F the interest is achieved by introducing slightly curved shapes firmly attached and held by the contrasting bold straight forms all placed at a slight angle.

6

EXAMPLES OF EXERCISES IN LAYOUT DESIGN

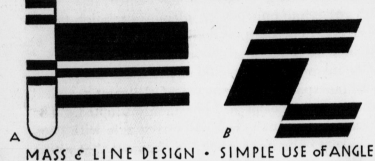

A   B

MASS & LINE DESIGN · SIMPLE USE of ANGLE

C   E

D

GEOMETRICALLY DESIGNED MASSES
INTRODUCING THE LINE · SPOT ·
PYRAMID · SEMICIRCLE & CURVE ·

F

IV. FITNESS FOR PURPOSE IN LAYOUT DESIGN

The planning and layout of lettering must be definitely related to the space or shape selected to contain it, just as the designing of a building must be considered in relation to the site on which it is to be built. Consideration of the space to be used is therefore of the first importance.

While lettering is used for many purposes, the simple upright rectangular space is found to be of the most practical use and is therefore the form most commonly adopted. The most usual text layout is the geometric rectangle with good margins as shown opposite. It will be observed that a true square is seldom used in book text or layout, as this shape is not so pleasing to the eye as the more elongated form.

THESE EXAMPLES illustrate that the weight and size of the mass layout should be fitted to the purpose for which it is intended, quite apart from the style of lettering used. The *title-page* may be light in weight and formal in character. The *sign* should be bolder because it must attract from a distance. The *newspaper advertisement* has a pictorial message and a large amount of text matter to be designed in a narrow space. The *address label* must be so designed as to leave a large area for a written address.

In the title-page opposite, as in all the examples, the most important factor is the value of white space or ground area. The title takes the prominent position and its legibility is emphasized by good margins. In the Bell sign the eye is immediately attracted to the word " Bell "; this is the most important feature as it explains the layout, and the decorative matter is secondary, yet the good use of spacing allows plenty of ground area and avoids a cramped appearance.

Fitness for purpose in Layout Design

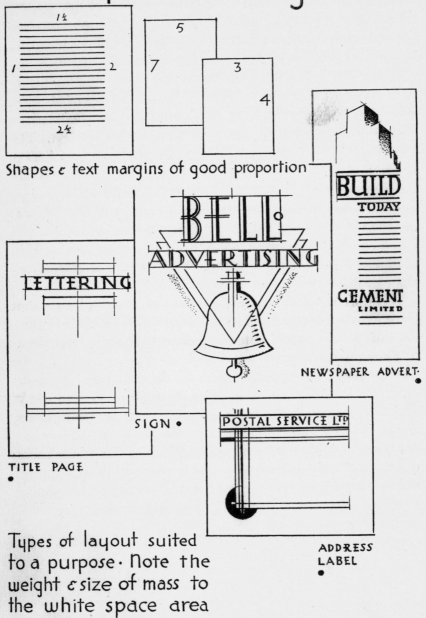

Shapes & text margins of good proportion

LETTERING

BELL ADVERTISING

BUILD TODAY CEMENT LIMITED

NEWSPAPER ADVERT·

SIGN ·

TITLE PAGE

POSTAL SERVICE LTD

ADDRESS LABEL

Types of layout suited to a purpose· Note the weight & size of mass to the white space area

V. FORMATION OF THE BASIC LETTERS

In commencing any study of lettering it is important to realize that all good modern European letter-forms have a common basic form, in that they have all been derived from the letters perfected by the Romans, who made the beautiful inscription on the Trajan Column. Moreover, the beginner must study the fundamental principles of letter making before attempting to create "fanciful" styles of lettering of his own.

Capitals are more often used than lower-case or small letters, and are simpler to form, so these will be discussed first. The Alphabet is formed of letters which are made either of entirely straight lines or of curved and straight lines combined; some letters occupy a true square and others are half a square in width. The letters built up in a square are: A C D G H N O Q T U V X Y Z, and the narrow letters based on a half-square are: B E F I J K L P R S. The two remaining letters of the alphabet, W and M, are slightly wider than a square.

It is the contrast between these wide and narrow letters that gives character and beauty to the finished word, and letters even of the very simplest forms must be of good proportion.

The skeleton letters on the opposite page show clearly the formation of the letters based on the square and those on the half-square. It must be emphasized that the letters M and W should always be wider than a square, and they may occupy a square and a half.

I and J, being letters of no width, must be spaced with great care in word-forming.

O C D
G Q A H
N T U V
X Y Z
B E F K L P R
S M W
I & J

FORMATION OF
THE BASIC
LETTERS

THESE ARE
FORMED ON
A CIRCLE
AND COVER
A SQUARE
AREA APPROX·

THESE ARE
BASED ON A
SQUARE·
WIDTH MAY BE
SLIGHTLY LESS·

THESE ARE
THE NARROW
LETTERS AND
SHOULD BE
APPROX· HALF
THE HEIGHT
IN WIDTH·

J MAY BE HALF
SQUARE IN WIDTH
OR EXTENDED
BELOW BASE LINE

ARE FORMED
WITH V SHAPE
& REQUIRE AREA
WIDER THAN SQ·

VI. MODERN BLOCK OR SERIF-LESS LETTERS

Block letters are the simplest type of capital letters derived from the skeleton form, and it will be seen that they are built up on the same proportions and are of equal thickness throughout. Known as *sans-serif* letters, because of the absence of serifs or shoulders, they are a most useful type for the designer as they are very legible and can be used for almost any subject. THE CHARACTER OF THE LETTER is determined by its weight and thickness. The letters shown in the middle section indicate a good proportion for general use, the thickness being approximately one-eleventh of its height. The size and weight used naturally depend entirely on the work in question and must be left to the judgment and discretion of the designer. The light-weight letters shown at the top of the page are a more elegant form, suitable for showcards and the lighter branches of display work. The bolder heavier letters are very compelling for posters or any subject where strong heavy lettering is required.

When the beginner first attempts to produce finished work he will find this a good type of lettering to adopt, but he must be aware of the inadvisability of making block letters his 'stock in trade.' It must be emphasized that the alphabets illustrated in this book are intended to serve as good guides for the beginner and must not merely be slavishly copied; the student should regard them as a basis on which to form his own letters, for they are shown principally to teach good proportions in the different types of alphabet.

ABC.

DEFGH
IJKLMN
OPQRS
TUVW
XYZ.

NOTE THE ALTERATION IN
CHARACTER BY MAKING THE
LETTERS LIGHT OR HEAVY.

2

VII. SPACING LETTERS TO FORM WORDS

It is well to remember that the ability to draw good letters efficiently is not enough: there must also be the ability to put the letters together to form words. Letters, however beautiful in themselves, must be arranged very carefully when formed into words or else they are of little value. The eye must be trained to space the letters with a feeling of rhythm or continuity when word-forming. This needs a good deal of thought and practice and until it is accomplished there can be no real sense of letter-planning.

METHOD OF SPACING

If letters are spaced into words mechanically, having the same *measured* distance between each letter, the result will appear either monotonous or disjointed and difficult to read. On the opposite page is an example of the right and wrong way of spacing the word ' water ': the first is obviously the right way with each letter spaced so as to give continuity and word completeness. This is achieved by balancing as equally as possible the full white space area that is allowed between each letter, disregarding any measured distance. Avoid any suggestion of cramped appearance or overcrowding of letters when word spacing, for this impairs legibility which is even more important than attractiveness.

RHYTHM

The lower examples illustrate the pattern made by that relation and repetition of straights and curves in lettering which produces rhythm. It is advisable to practise with a round-nibbed pen simple exercises similar to those given here in order to appreciate the existence of rhythm. Such exercises lead also to a freedom in forming good letters and good spacing.

14

THE RIGHT AND WRONG METHOD OF
SPACING LETTERS TO FORM WORDS.

WATER
WHITE SPACE AREA BALANCED — RIGHT

WATER
MEASURED DISTANCE | DITTO | DITTO | DITTO — WRONG

FOUR EXERCISES WITH
THE PEN TO PRODUCE
RHYTHM•

MOTOR
SPOR
MOTOR

LONDON
LONDON
LONDON

SOLS
SOLS
SOLS

PORTFOLIO

VIII. HOW TO USE THE TOOLS TO CONSTRUCT LETTERS

It is well to become familiar with the right use of T square and set square for the preliminary setting out on paper or board. The illustration on the opposite page indicates how they should be used to ensure the obtaining of true horizontal and vertical lines.

HOW TOOLS INFLUENCE LETTER PRODUCTION.

It will be found that the tool employed in the making of a letter will influence considerably the character and style.

The two types of lettering with which we are concerned are:

1. Letters that are directly drawn with the tool— *i.e.*, produced with the script pen or one-stroke brush, where the character is very dependent on the right use of tool.
2. Built-up letters, where the shape is built up in outline with the pencil, pen or brush, and then filled in. This type largely depends on the taste and knowledge of the designer for its good form, and necessitates the study of good models past and present.

In the upper examples on the opposite page it will be seen that if the pen or brush, with its chisel edge, is held in a constant slant position and is made to follow the shape of the basic letter, it will naturally produce a letter of good character, with the thick and thin strokes, curves and serifs.

In the " built-up " letters it will be noticed that they follow the basic form and are shown partly completed. While these letters can be made with either pen or brush or both, the tool should still influence the character, as will be seen in the brush-formed Roman letter which appears freely drawn.

It is a mistake to use instruments too rigidly in letter making, as this tends to give them a mechanical appearance.

The formation of the serif of the Roman letter indicates the proportion of curve best employed.

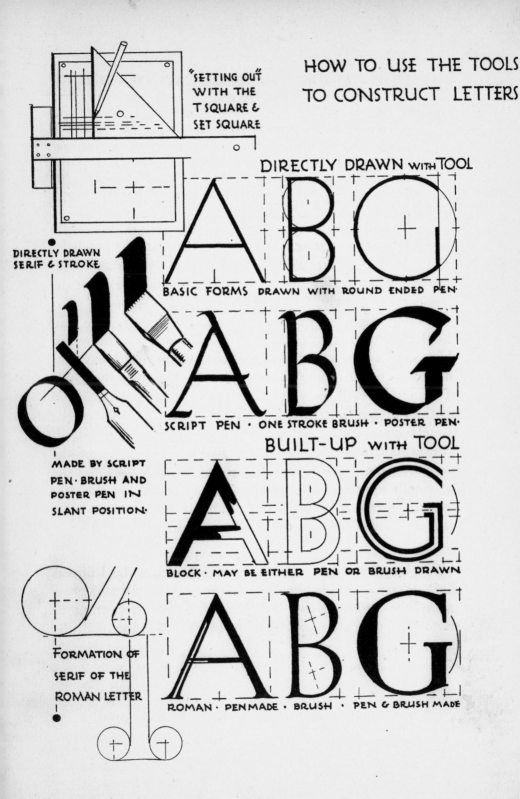

"SETTING OUT"
WITH THE
T SQUARE &
SET SQUARE

DIRECTLY DRAWN with TOOL

DIRECTLY DRAWN
SERIF & STROKE

BASIC FORMS DRAWN WITH ROUND ENDED PEN

MADE BY SCRIPT
PEN · BRUSH AND
POSTER PEN IN
SLANT POSITION·

SCRIPT PEN · ONE STROKE BRUSH · POSTER PEN·

BUILT-UP WITH TOOL

BLOCK · MAY BE EITHER PEN OR BRUSH DRAWN

FORMATION OF
SERIF OF THE
ROMAN LETTER

ROMAN · PEN MADE · BRUSH · PEN & BRUSH MADE

IX. MODERN ROMAN CAPITALS

This is a brush-drawn alphabet, copied from the original which was chisel-carved by the Romans. It is the basis of all our present-day styles, for it is the most perfect in shape, proportion and balance. The designer should know and draw this type of alphabet because a thorough knowledge of it will enable him to adapt it as a foundation for all the modern letters he cares to create.

PROPORTION AND CHARACTER

The Roman letters are built up on the square and half-square. The importance of these proportions cannot be stressed too strongly, for a great deal of the beauty of these letters depends upon them. The beginner must realize that the thick or wide part of the letter is obtained by adding this thickness on the *inside* of the foundation shape, as for example in the case of the letter O the thickness is drawn on the inside of the circle. All the vertical or down strokes are thick and all the horizontal strokes are thin; the contrast between the two thicknesses must be apparent but not over-emphasized. The proportions opposite give a very suitable scale of the weight for the size of letter; of course, the larger the letter the heavier it must be in weight, but always avoid too strong a contrast—nothing looks worse than Roman letters which have very thick down-strokes and very thin horizontals.

SERIFS

To give their letters a pleasing completeness the Romans designed serifs or shoulders. These must be small and grow out of the letter. Never let the serifs be too important or the whole character and dignity of the alphabet will be destroyed.

DEFGH

ABC

IJKLM

NOPQ

RSTU

VWXYZ

X. CAPITALS FORMED WITH THE SCRIPT PEN

Letters produced with the slant script pen were used extensively throughout Europe for illuminated manuscripts and books during the great manuscript period from the eighth to the fifteenth centuries before the advent of the printing press. The present-day uses of this lettering are for illuminated addresses and hand-written books and, in advertising, for quickly produced showcards, for ticket-writing and similar display.

TOOLS.

This type of letter can be produced with:

1. The quill or reed (which can be cut to size and steel reservoir added).
2. Modern steel script nib (obtainable in all sizes).
3. Poster pen (for large commercial work).
4. The one-stroke brush (as used by the sign writer).

For the beginner the steel script pen with a reservoir attachment to hold the ink is the best tool with which to practise.

MATERIALS.

Smooth paper is the best for working on, and an ' unfixed ' India ink with a filler attachment.

. A medium soft pencil may be used for guide lines, after which the letters must be freely drawn with the pen.

HOW TO PRODUCE THE LETTERS.

The student is advised to use a fairly broad nib to commence with. The alphabet on the opposite page indicates the width of strokes and therefore the size of nib suitable for this scale of letter. The pen must be held in a writing position and the edge of the nib must always be held at an angle of 45° to the horizontal. This automatically produces the thick and thin strokes. The top alphabet is the simplest type to produce, and is good for general use. The alternative alphabet is based on an Early English form. The student is advised to practise forming strokes with the pen—downstrokes, diagonal strokes, curves and serifs—then the letter forms and the forming of words.

Script pen Lettering

Capitals formed with the slanted script pen

A B C D E F G
A H I J K L M
N O P Q
R S T

Alternative alphabet of rounder form

A B D E F G
h k m r
P S T U n

U V W
X Y Z &

Formal serifs

B D h L r

XI. LOWER-CASE LETTERS FORMED WITH THE SCRIPT PEN

These lower-case or small letters are for use with the script pen capitals. Originally only capital letters were used, but the small letters came into being through the necessity of writing capitals more quickly, so that a definite variant was developed. Examples on the opposite page show a modern-ized form of the early mediæval script pen-made letter. From this style of lettering modern bush-formed lower-case and printers' type were developed. The chief advantage of the small letters is that a larger amount of text can be arranged in the space available. Also, they have great decorative value when used together with capitals. The tools are the same as those used for making the capitals and the pen must be held at the same angle.

SPACING

As some of these letters have stems which project above and below the line, known as 'ascenders' and 'descenders,' allowance for these must be made when spacing, otherwise the descenders of one line will become confused with the ascenders of the other.

WORD FORMING

When forming words with the small letters each letter should be close to its neighbour and in some cases may connect to give continuity and solidity. It is advisable to acquire a good round form of letter for good character and legibility. As in the case of the making of capitals, practice is necessary to produce a good hand, and exercises such as short notices, simple showcards, etc., should be attempted, using both lower-case and capital letters.

Slant Pen Small Letters

abcdefg
hijklmno
pqrstuv

A Modern Formal Type

wxyz abcdefgg
hijklmno
pqrstuw
vxyz:

The Numerals
&123456789

XII. ROMAN LOWER-CASE LETTERS

The lower-case Roman letter is directly derived from the pen-made form and is a generally recognised form of letter used for present-day lettering and printing purposes. The lower-case letters on the opposite page are designed for use with the Roman brush-formed capitals on page 19; they have the same characteristics, such as a good round form of the curved letters and similar proportions of the thick and thin strokes together with the use of serif finishings.

SPACING

In spacing out this type of letter the same care must be taken as in the production of capitals. When the size of letter has been ascertained the guide lines must be ruled sufficiently wide apart to allow room for the ascending and descending parts of each letter. Four lines of equal distance apart are necessary for each row of lettering, the two middle ones for the body of the letter, the one above to determine the height of the ascending stems and the one below for the descending stems.

FORMATION AND USE

As these are ' built-up ' letters they must first be arranged and drawn in pencil, then outlined and filled in with the brush as in the Roman capitals. To obtain good character, care should be taken when branching the curves for the straights. This is a very clear and legible letter and of practical value to the designer. Although usually used as secondary lettering in conjunction with capitals, well-drawn lower-case can be distinctive and beautiful.

lower
case
letters of
• ROMAN
form

a b c d e

R f g h i j l

A k o m n

o p q r s t

u v w

x y z

XIII. ITALIC: SCRIPT PEN AND BRUSH FORMED

A graceful and elegant type of letter, it is particularly distinctive on account of its freely made appearance and less formal character. It was originally evolved as a form of cursive writing with the pen and was perfected in Italy in the first half of the sixteenth century.

Whilst italic closely resembles the roman letter, both upper- and lower-case, and can therefore be used in conjunction with both, its essential features are:

1. The slightly narrowed width of letter.
2. The setting of the letters at a slight slope to the right.
3. The freely made appearance and lightness of weight.

The slight narrowness of the letters makes it possible to arrange more words to the line, and italic can therefore be usefully employed when economy of space is a consideration. The slope of the letter makes it possible to produce italic easily and rapidly, especially with the slant pen. It assists the branching of the curves from the straights, making them appear easy and less angular, and helps to give clearance at the junction of the strokes.

Script pen italic should be made freely with a slanted pen of a medium size. The ascending and descending strokes of lower-case will be slightly elongated, while the descenders can be slightly curved or flourished. In setting out, the guide lines must be more widely spaced to allow for this elongation.

Brush-drawn italics must be arranged and drawn in pencil, then completed with a brush or pen as a built-up letter. To obtain the freely made quality essential to the character of the italic letter, it is advisable to practise with the script pen as much as possible before attempting to produce a brush-formed type.

Italic is useful in general for prefaces, marginal notes, poems or quotations, for emphasis, or simply for an effect of free elegance.

Italic: Script Pen

abcdef ABCE
ghijkstl FGHSL
mnopqr
wxyz and Brush Formed
abcde
fghij
ABCDEFGHI

XIV. FLOURISHED CAPITALS AND NUMERALS

A purely decorative letter that can be used with considerable advantage when lettering is to be considered as decoration. It is often used in conjunction with lower-case italic in the form of initial letters. As the name implies, the letters are freely made with the pen or brush, with the forms and terminals extended or flourished. They are also known as 'swash' letters, a name given them by the printers of the seventeenth century who modelled some of their types on this form.

There can be no definite rule for the actual formation of the letters, as they are made freely at the will or the discretion of the designer to suit his requirements. They usually take the form of drawn-out letters, or letters with width added and extensions flourished as marginal decorations. It is advisable, however, to retain as much as possible of the basic roman shape so that they remain legible. The examples given opposite are comparatively simple and will serve as good models.

THE NUMERALS known as 'Arabic,' from their Eastern origin, have developed into the definitely recognised figures accepted today. Until the fifteenth century the letters M D C L X V and I were used to express numerals. These examples are designed for use with the roman capitals.

It is generally essential that the arrangement and weight of the thick and thin strokes and the making of serifs should harmonize or be consistent with the type of letter employed.

THE EXAMPLES OF DECORATIVE LINE FINISHINGS and borders are intended to illustrate the variety of simple decorative effects that can be produced with the slant script pen. It is advisable to practise the making of simple decoration with pen and brush, as it will be found that decoration will more readily harmonize with lettering if tools and materials employed are the same.

FLOURISHED LETTERS

ALGHBR
VQ1

SCRIPT.

Decorative line
finishings &
borders

2345
6789
0

BRUSH   NUMERALS

BRUSH FORM

GRABN
WF

XV. GRADED EXERCISES FOR SCHOOLS AND BEGINNERS

The foregoing pages have been designed primarily to aid the beginner, and should therefore be of value as a basis of study for the subject of lettering and its practice in schools and by private students. It will be found that interest in lettering will be sustained when applied to exercises in design and pattern making, which stimulate the imagination and give scope for the inventive faculties.

This page has been included to help the beginner to apply lettering to a practical use, and to illustrate some interesting types of graded exercises that can be carried out while the various basic styles of lettering are being learnt. It is important to commence with the planning of the layout before attempting any actual finished work.

1. *Skeleton roman* produced with round-nibbed pen. First try arranging lines of letters or words of different sizes together with simple decorative motives, spots, borders, etc. Many decorative uses can be found, such as Christmas cards, nursery rhymes, charts, simple embroideries, etc.

2. *Block lettering* is useful for encouraging good craftsmanship, spacing and legibility. It can be attractively used with colour for such things as pages for illustrated alphabets, simple notices, posters and lino-cuts.

3. *Roman capitals* are perhaps the most difficult letters to produce well, therefore simple arrangements of a few words should be first attempted. Names on book-covers or book-plates, house names and headings for important notices.

4. *Script lettering* is usually found easier to produce than roman, so that exercises in this form of lettering might well be attempted at an early stage. It can be used to advantage for quickly written notices, for posters, invitations, menus, etc.

5. *Italic flourished letters* and other decorative varieties are fascinating in use for wall inscriptions, maps, etc.

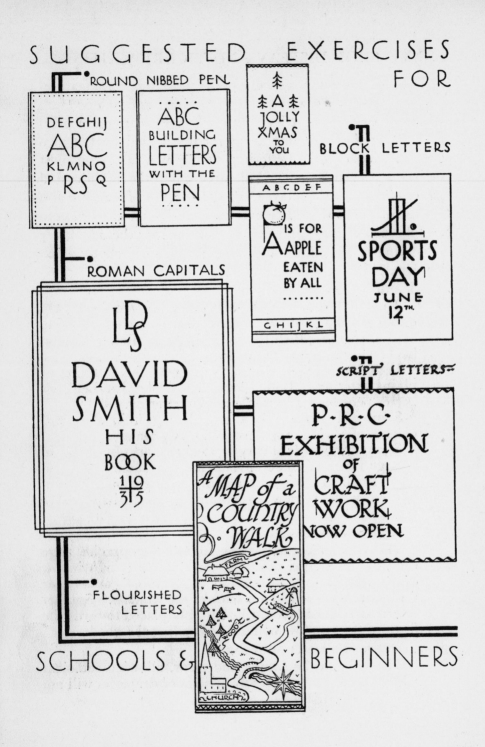

SUGGESTED EXERCISES FOR

ROUND NIBBED PEN

DEFGHIJ
ABC
KLMNO
P RS Q

ABC
BUILDING
LETTERS
WITH THE
PEN

A
JOLLY
XMAS
TO
YOU

BLOCK LETTERS

ABCDEF
A IS FOR
APPLE
EATEN
BY ALL
GHIJKL

SPORTS
DAY
JUNE 12TH.

ROMAN CAPITALS

LDS
DAVID
SMITH
HIS
BOOK
19
3 5

SCRIPT LETTERS

P·R·C·
EXHIBITION
OF
CRAFT
WORK
NOW OPEN

A MAP of a
COUNTRY
WALK

FLOURISHED
LETTERS

SCHOOLS & BEGINNERS

XVI. SHOP DISPLAY AND TICKET WRITING

The shop window is now one of the most important features of the modern store, and window dressing has developed into an art of itself. Attractively lettered showcards and displays are among the most important mediums used by the progressive shopkeeper. Lettering, acting as a salesman, must deliver a sales message and call attention to the qualities and prices of the goods displayed. Type and size of lettering and the use of colour should be carefully considered in relation to an intended display, and the style of lettering should convey something of the nature and quality of the objects to which it refers.

TOOLS AND MATERIALS.

Ruler, T square and set square are required. On dark coloured cards or painted surfaces, a chalked string held in position, then lightly pulled and allowed to snap back, will give white guide lines.

Lettering brushes: Red sable (riggers) for outlining or plain lettering. Camel-hair one-stroke brushes and poster pens for rapid single-stroke lettering.

Showcard white, black and Indian ink, showcard colours of a wide range are sold ready for use.

Showcard boards of varying thickness are obtainable in a large range of colours; these are of standard size, and when small sizes are required the cutting should be considered with a view to obtaining good shapes with economy.

POSITION OF WINDOW CARDS.

The small diagram at the top of the opposite page suggests some good positions for showcards in window display. The chief position for a " feature " card is near the centre and well to the back of the window. Smaller informative cards should be suitably placed towards the front of the window without concealing the goods.

PRICE-TICKETS AND SMALL SHOWCARDS.

These should be simple and clear, allowing sufficient white space area so that any articles or draperies will not hide the information.

LETTERING FOR SHOP DISPLAY

12½ *Royal Showcard*
20" X 25"

20"

10"   10"

6¼"

12½   5"
6¼"

CUTTING SHOWCARD TO
OBTAIN GOOD SHAPES

A
B
C   D

A FEATURE CARD
B INFORMATION
C LIST OF PRICES
D REMINDER

GOOD DISPLAY POSITIONS FOR
SHOWCARDS

K STORE
2'7'6

AVOID A CRAMPED
APPEARANCE IN
PRICE TICKETS

BEST
COAL
45'

Gifts
for men

COAT
WEEK
Special offer for
this week only

This New
RADIO
14 GNS.

Leander Ltd
MODEL
GOWNS

& TICKET WRITING

XVII. LAYOUT FOR SHOP DISPLAY AND TICKET WRITING

TYPES OF LETTERING.

For most purposes in showcard work the lettering and matter should be sufficiently interesting in themselves, so that elaborate illustration and decoration should not be required. Good block and roman lettering will be found valuable for conveying the sales message in a clear and tasteful manner. The one-stroke brush lettering will be found useful when a large amount of lettering is required, or when several cards or tickets are needed for one display. With practice this type of lettering can be produced very rapidly. When endeavouring to create new styles of letters it is advisable to commence by making modifications on existing styles.

LAYOUT FOR DISPLAY.

For good advertising it is essential to be interesting. With imagination, and some ability to design, attractive display showcards and the like can be produced simply at very little cost. With a good layout simple illustrations or symbols, decoratively treated, can convey an idea or act as decoration. The suitability of the type of lettering and layout should always be considered in relation to the type of commodity advertised: for instance, a freely designed showcard with italic lettering would be suitable for a florist or for ladies' hosiery, whereas a bold design with block or heavy form of lettering might well be used where strength and stability are important factors.

Colour attracts if it appeals as a colour scheme. Attractive displays can be achieved with tinted cards, especially where there is little colour in the commodities displayed.

Cut-out showcards can be devised to make interesting complete shapes by arranging the design so that parts of the card can be removed.

Display stands of a semi-permanent nature can be very effectively and simply made with coloured cards for lettering to form background, held together with shelves of card or wood, for display of small articles.

34

SUGGESTED LAYOUTS

Belgrave for Flowers

SHOW
CARDS
OR

Spring Sale

WINDOW
BILLS

SUITS PRESSED & CLEANED 4/6

DISPLAY
STANDS

SEE THE NEW REPAIR SERVICE

2/1 RAIN COAT

'CUTOUT'
SHOWCARDS

FOR SHOP   DISPLAY

XVIII. LETTERING AND LAYOUT FOR COMMERCIAL ART

The outstanding essential of modern advertising publicity is skilful presentation of information with the object of selling. The work of the commercial artist is to deliver the sales message by means of pictorial matter and lettering, and he therefore produces drawings that can be reproduced by one of the mechanical methods of printing.

When the nature of the advertisement has been decided the artist designs draft schemes suggesting the various intended components, pictorial matter, captions, type matter and drawn lettering. This is known as preparing layouts. On the originality and suitability of these designs largely depends the ultimate success of the finished advertisement. It is therefore advisable to practise layout design as much as possible. Attributive colour work is very essential and should be carefully studied.

LETTERING FOR REPRODUCTION.

Although much can be expressed by pictorial matter, lettering is necessary to convey the message. Type can be used to great advantage, but hand-drawn lettering is extensively used because of its flexibility in adaptation. It can be designed to form an integral part of a design, and its character and form can be drawn in harmony with the rest of the pictorial matter. A high standard of clear precision is required in all lettering drawn for reproduction, because it must be photographed for transference to block, and it may be used in conjunction with types which are clear and sharp. It is usual to draw lettering larger than required, as it will appear sharper when reduced and reproduced.

With present-day advertising taking so many various and original forms it must obviously give considerable scope for the designing of new types and styles of lettering. Nevertheless new types can only be satisfactorily produced through the knowledge and study of good existing models.

The careful study of the many good type faces will be found to be valuable, both from the point of view of designing and because type must often be selected and used in an advertisement. Compiling reference-lists of various kinds of lettering and types will be of great assistance.

TOOLS AND MATERIALS.

Accuracy is important in drawing for reproduction: T squares, set squares, rulers, compasses should all be accurate.

Drawing pens. Ruling pens for straight lines.

Good sable brushes of various sizes.

Fixed Indian ink for black and white work.

Process white for use where white is not intended to photograph.

Poster colours usually used for flat colour work.

Cartridge drawing paper for layouts, etc.

Bristol board for black-and-white work.

Water-colour board for colour work.

EXAMPLES OF LAYOUT.

The next three pages of illustrations demonstrate some of the important methods of layout design that can be applied to advertising. They are designed to suggest and emphasize the various effects and qualities achieved by definite arrangement. They are drawn in the form of preliminary layouts showing the related components. The pictorial matter is suggested very simply. The size, character and position of important lettering is shown and the type copy matter indicated by a series of ruled lines in rectangular shapes.

Examples A, B and C (page 39) show three simple and compact arrangements to obtain unity and balance. Note the value of surrounding white space ground area contained in each. This has been emphasized.

Example D (page 40) indicates how a geometrical composition can form a basis for layout and be useful for suggesting original designs. E demonstrates the value of simplicity in arrangement where distinction and quality are desired.

Example F (page 41) shows how the entire space can be utilized by a bold arrangement of lettering only. G is an example of narrow space arrangement of several sections of copy held together by an illustration or line giving a slant movement and helping to carry the eye through. H is a free-style layout where a freely drawn illustration, type and other matter have to be arranged in one design. Note how the free use of lettering helps to connect them.

TYPES OF LETTERING FOR ADVERTISING (PAGES 42-43).

These pages illustrate the possibilities of this type of design and show that letters can be designed to convey a definite impression suitable to the words employed. This is a form of symbolism, and with this in mind many original arrangements and types can be evolved. The weight, form and character should be consistent throughout each set of letters or word designed. Nevertheless, remember that good sans-serif and roman lettering will always convey a legible message.

GOOD TYPE FACES (PAGE 44).

Garamond Bold.—A good display face for bold advertisements and for relief lines in display work.

Garamond.—A book face suitable for delicate advertising—*e.g.*, feminine commodities.

Bodoni.—An eighteenth-century type. Good for display and title-pages. Brilliant.

Baskerville.—A book face, clean cut.

Caslon.—A good standard type; a foundation letter good to copy.

Perpetua.—A clear modern titling designed on classic lines.

Forum.—Closely formed on pure Roman capitals. A titling face, having no lower-case. Useful for high-class jobbing work, invitation cards, etc.

Gill Sans Light.—A lighter face suitable for general advertising.

Gill Sans Bold.—Designed by Eric Gill, a good legible modern type for bold advertising.

BALANCE

CENTRE LINE

CENTRE LINE
BALANCED
LAYOUT

Examples of Layout
For Advertising

unity

ARRANGEMENT OF
TYPE AND DRAWN
LETTERING TO
ACHIEVE UNITY

LARGE
AND SMALL

COMPONENTS

A BALANCED
DESIGN WITH
COMPONENTS of
VARYING SIZE

EXAMPLES of LAYOUT FOR ADVERTISING.

GEOMETRIC DESIGNS

LAYOUT SUITABLE FOR
FOLDER-COVER BUILT
UP ON GEOMETRICAL BASIS

SIMPLICITY

MOTORS

DISTINCTION ACHIEVED BY SIMPLE
LAYOUT AND USE OF WHITE SPACE

40

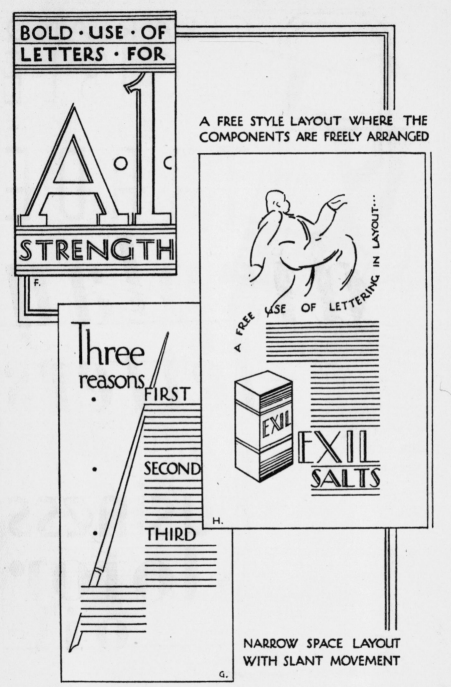

BOLD · USE · OF
LETTERS · FOR
A1
STRENGTH

F.

A FREE STYLE LAYOUT WHERE THE
COMPONENTS ARE FREELY ARRANGED

A FREE USE OF LETTERING IN LAYOUT···

EXIL
EXIL
SALTS

H.

Three
reasons
• FIRST
• SECOND
• THIRD

G.

NARROW SPACE LAYOUT
WITH SLANT MOVEMENT

CLEAR AND

LEGIBLE

TRADE

display

letters

Elegant and free

business

Motor

SUMMER

WINTER

oil=

TYPES OF LETTERING

42

ROMAN

QUALITY + HONESTY

Fashion ltd.

GRACE

and beauty

Frolic some

TWEED

POWER

R

OR ADVERTISING

43

GARAMOND bold 1 2 3 4 5 6 7 8 9

GARAMOND bold italic 1 2 3 4 5 6

GARAMOND 24-point 1 2 3 4 5 6 7 8 9 0

BODONI 24-point 1 2 3 4 5 6 7 8 9 0

BASKERVILLE 24-point 1 2 3 4 5 6 7 8 9 0

CASLON old face 1 2 3 4 5 6 7 8 9 0

PERPETUA 24-POINT 1 2 3 4 5 6 7 8 9 0

FORUM 24-POINT 1 2 3 4 5 6 7 8 9

GILL SANS SERIF serif 1 2 3 4 5 6 7

GILL SANS BOLD bold 1 2 3 4 5 6

44

Date Due

BROADMAN
B P
SUPPLIES

Code 4386-04, CLS-4, Broadman Supplies, Nashville, Tenn.,
Printed in U.S.A.